THE SPIRITUALS COLLECTION

Cover photo © William Koechling/Getty Images

— PIANO LEVEL —
LATE INTERMEDIATE/EARLY ADVANCED

ISBN 978-1-4234-7610-8

HAL•LEONARD® CORPORATION

7777 W. BLUEMOUND RD. P.O. BOX 13819 MILWAUKEE, WI 53213

In Australia Contact:
Hal Leonard Australia Pty. Ltd.
4 Lentara Court
Cheltenham, Victoria, 3192 Australia
Email: ausadmin@halleonard.com.au

Visit Hal Leonard Online at
www.halleonard.com

Visit Phillip at
www.phillipkeveren.com

PREFACE

Spirituals come from the period of slavery in America. They communicate the pain of the slave's predicament, and the joy born from a faith in a better life after death. These rich tunes are simple, yet profoundly moving.

Spirituals have influenced countless classical and popular composers. Some believe that they are the very foundation for what later became jazz. Jazz musicians turn to them for improvisational material. People all around the world find joy and inspiration in them.

These settings for piano solo were written with a deep admiration for the beauty of the source material. I hope you enjoy playing them.

Sincerely,
Phillip Keveren

BIOGRAPHY

Phillip Keveren, a multi-talented keyboard artist and composer, has composed original works in a variety of genres from piano solo to symphonic orchestra. Mr. Keveren gives frequent concerts and workshops for teachers and their students in the United States, Canada, Europe, and Asia. Mr. Keveren holds a B.M. in composition from California State University Northridge and a M.M. in composition from the University of Southern California.

CONTENTS

ALL MY TRIALS

African-American Spiritual
Arranged by Phillip Keveren

Rubato

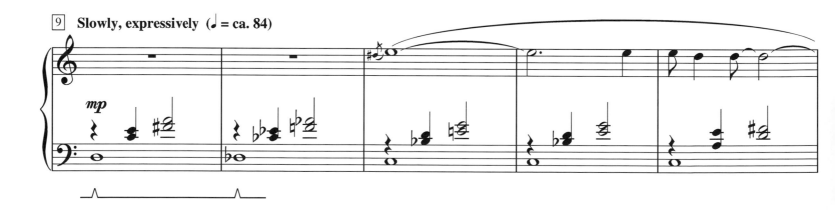

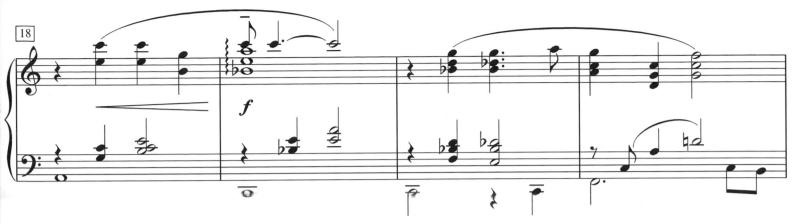

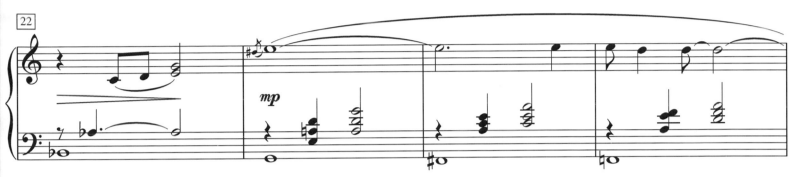

Rubato

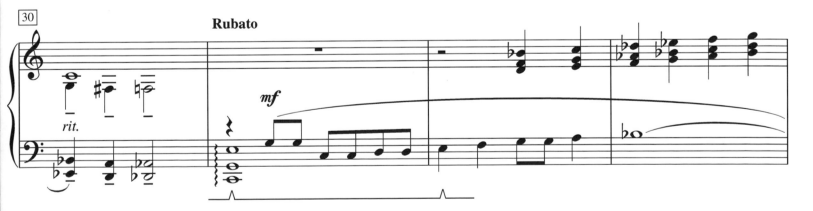

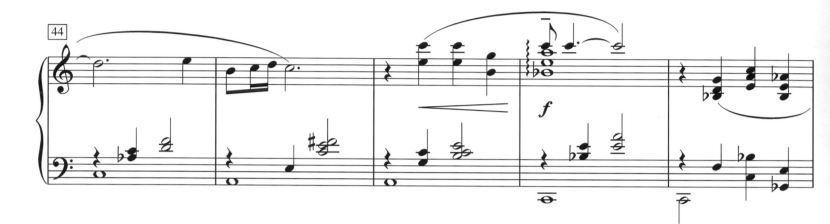

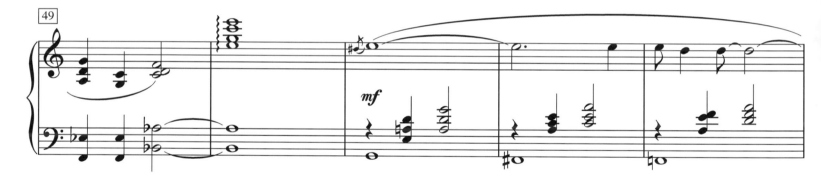

DEEP RIVER

African-American Spiritual
Based on Joshua 3
Arranged by Phillip Keveren

Longingly ($\quad$ = 76)

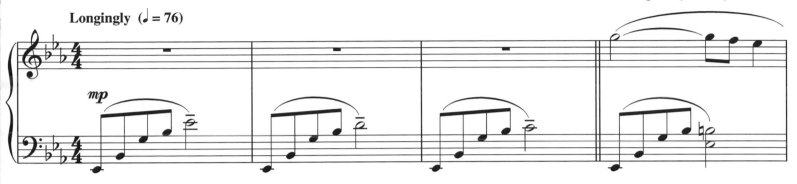

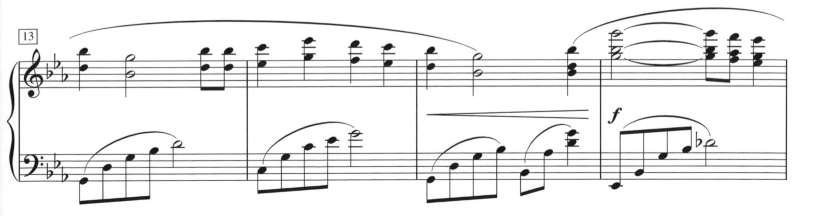

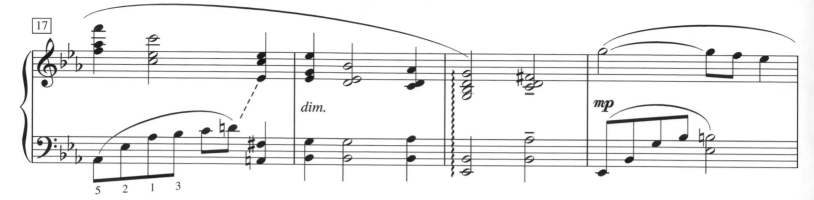

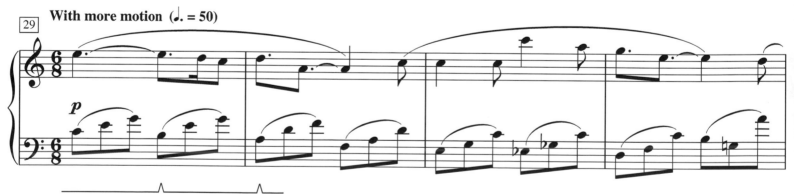

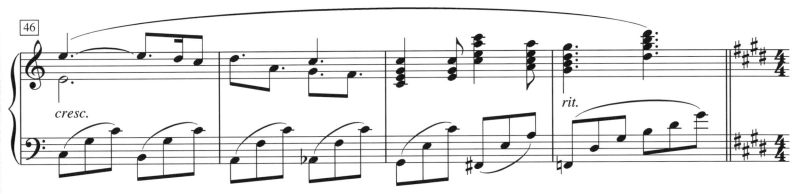

Tempo I

EVERY TIME I FEEL THE SPIRIT

African-American Spiritual
Arranged by Phillip Keveren

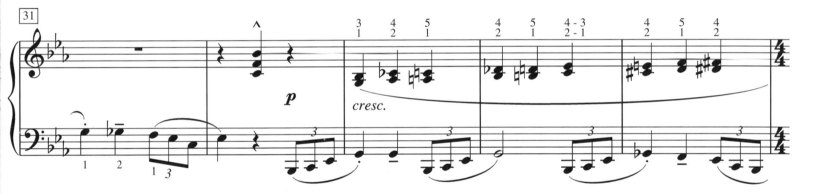

HE'S GOT THE WHOLE WORLD IN HIS HANDS

Traditional Spiritual
Arranged by Phillip Keveren

Tenderly, with rubato (♩ = 88)

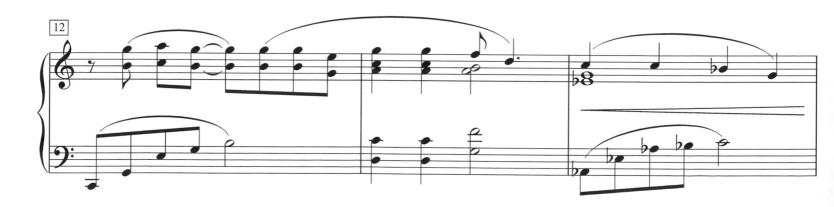

Swing (♩ = 108)

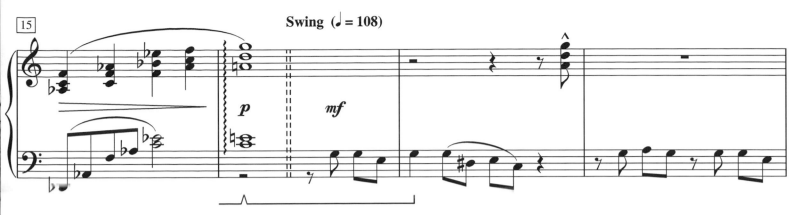

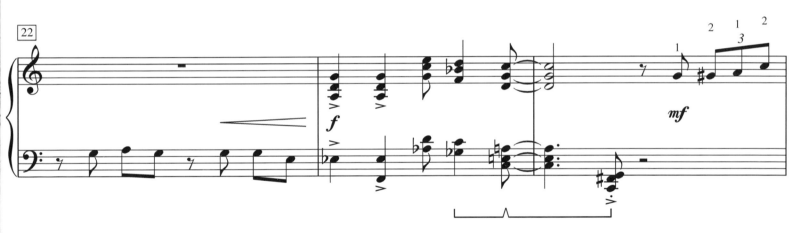

JOSHUA
(Fit the Battle of Jericho)

African-American Spiritual
Arranged by Phillip Keveren

Moderately slow, freely (♩ = ca. 108)

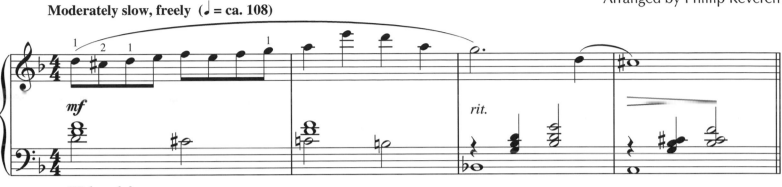

With pedal

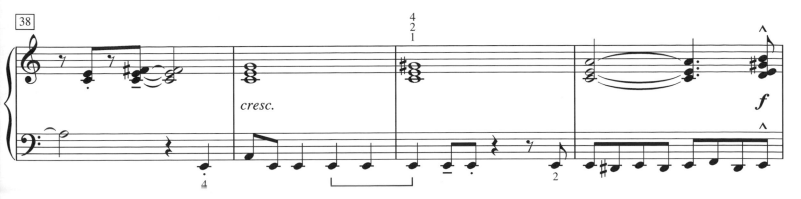

WE ARE CLIMBING JACOB'S LADDER

African-American Spiritual
Arranged by Phillip Keveren

Lento (♩ = 66)

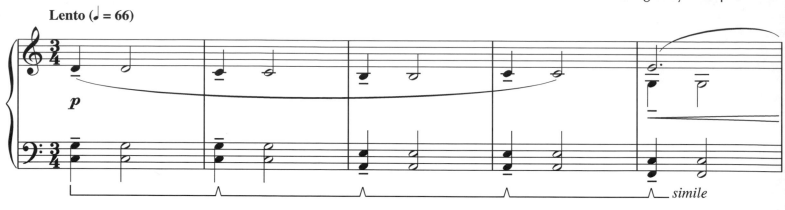

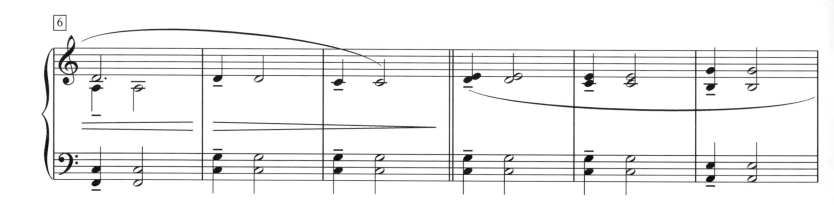

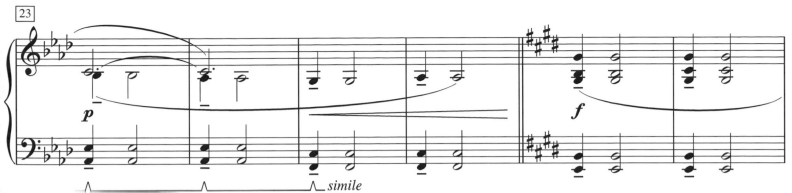

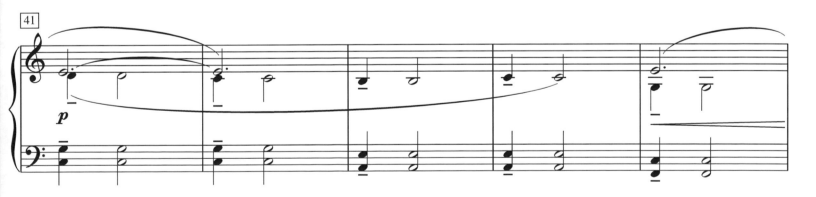

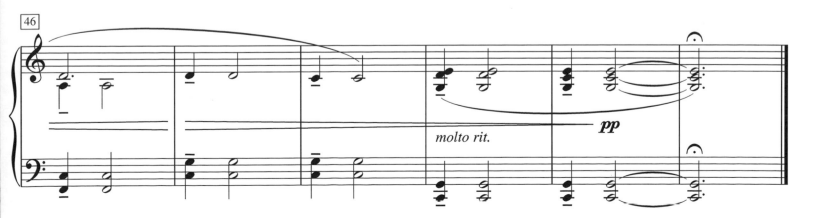

LET US BREAK BREAD TOGETHER

Traditional Spiritual
Arranged by Phillip Keveren

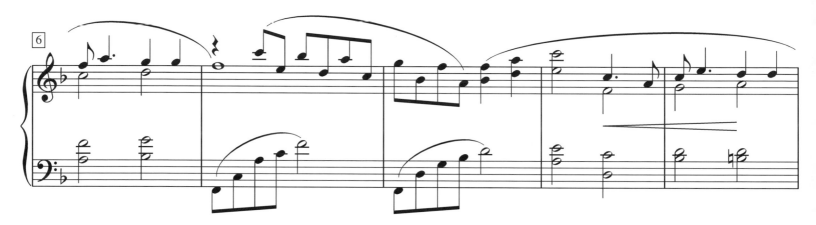

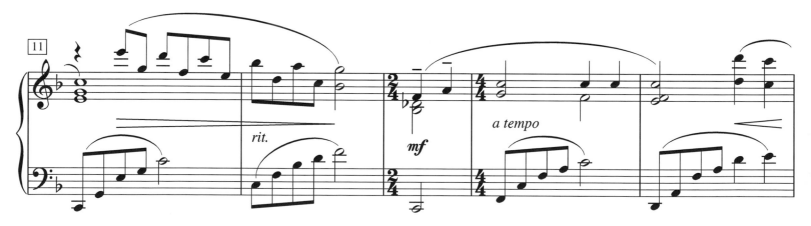

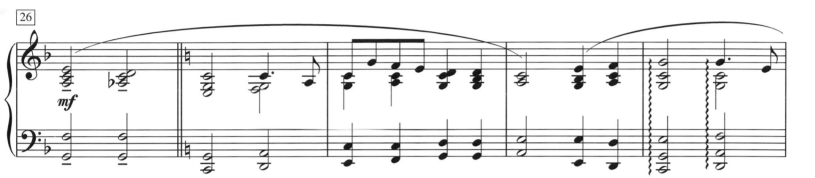

THE LONESOME ROAD

African-American Spiritual
Arranged by Phillip Keveren

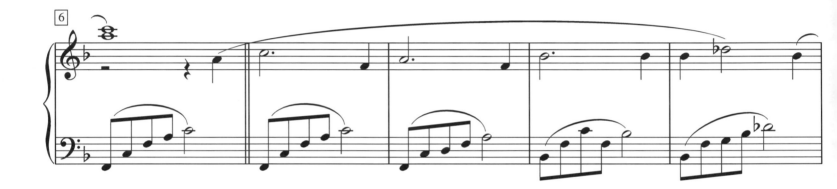

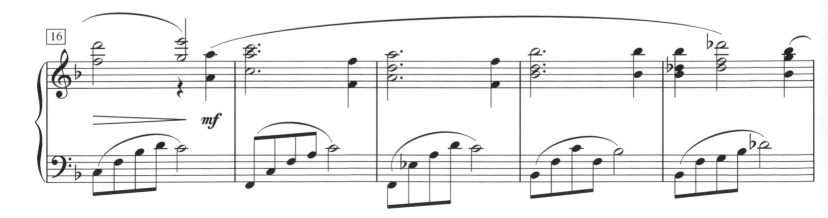

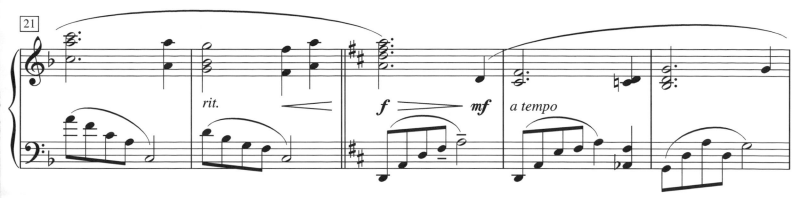

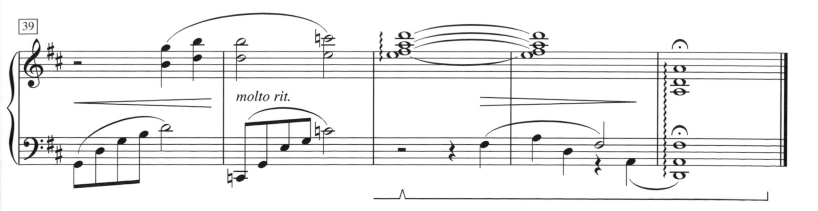

SOMEBODY'S KNOCKIN' AT YOUR DOOR

African-American Spiritual
Arranged by Phillip Keveren

Lively (♩ = 126)

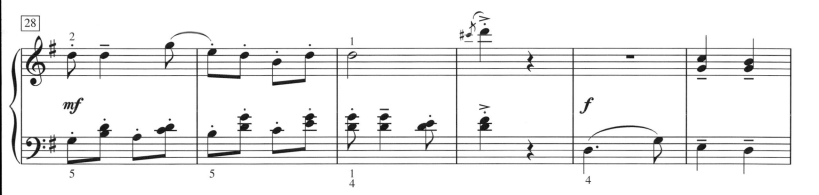

Slowly, freely (♩ = 96–100)

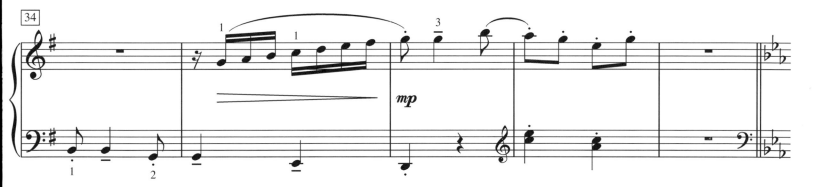

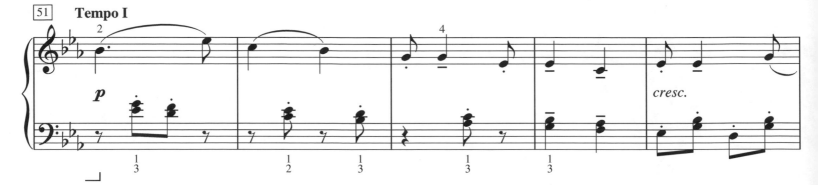

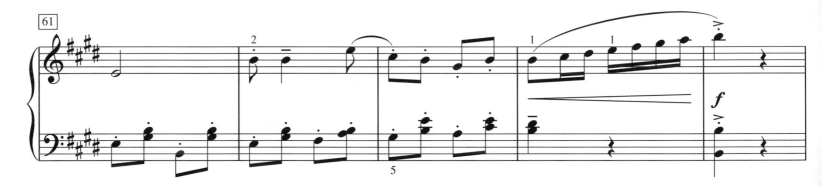

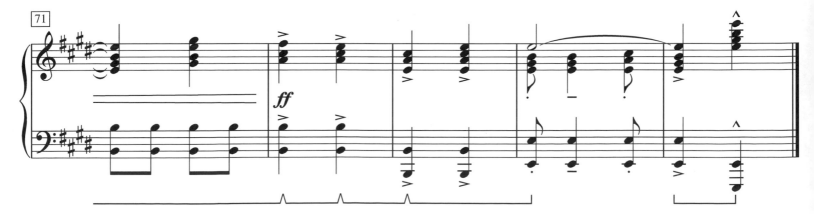

SWING LOW, SWEET CHARIOT

Traditional Spiritual
Arranged by Phillip Keveren

Freely, with deep expression (♩ = 72)

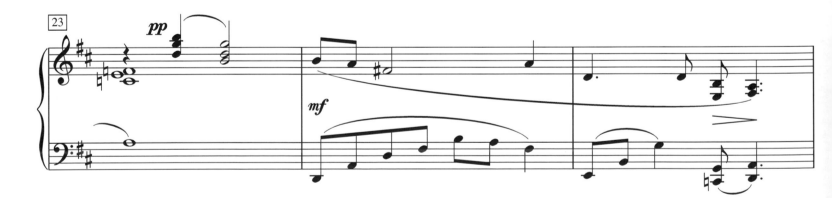

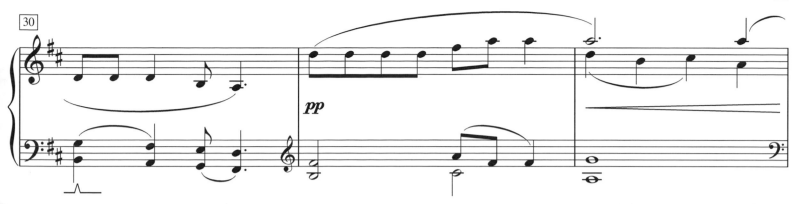

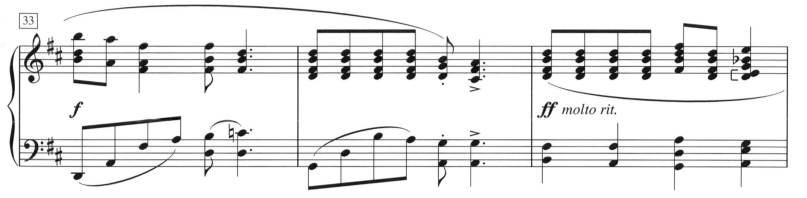

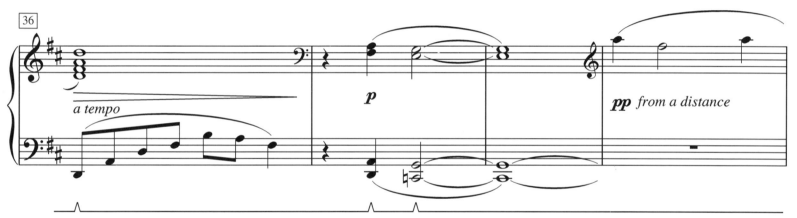

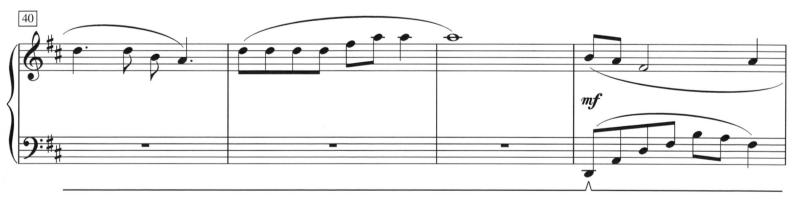

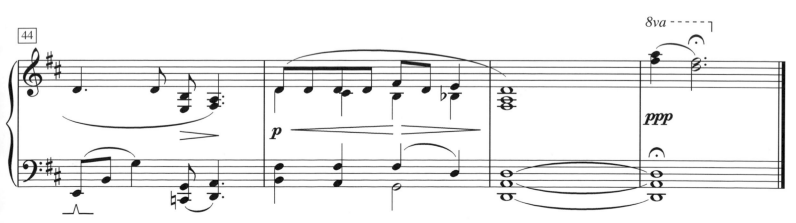

SOMETIMES I FEEL LIKE A MOTHERLESS CHILD

African-American Spiritual
Arranged by Phillip Keveren

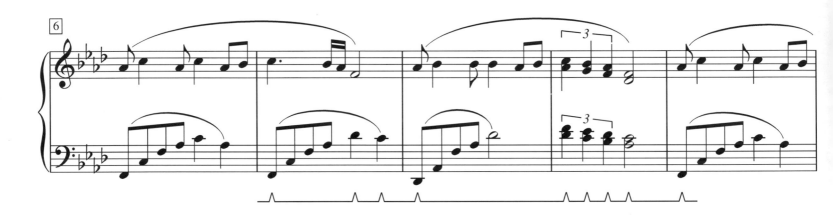

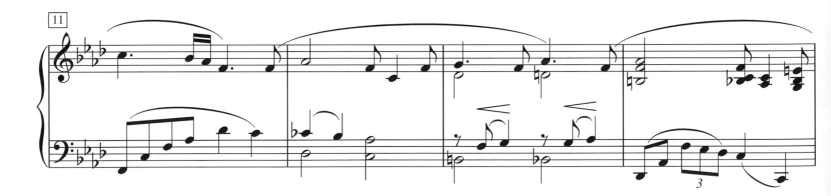

STEAL AWAY
(Steal Away to Jesus)

Traditional Spiritual
Arranged by Phillip Keveren

Deeply expressive (♩ = 76-84)

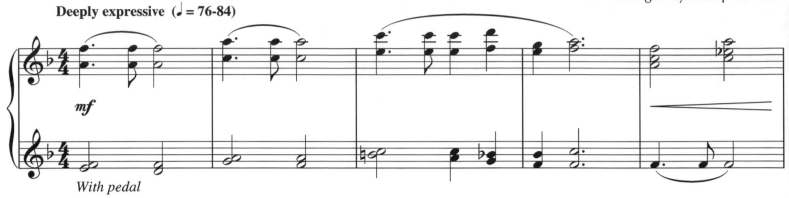

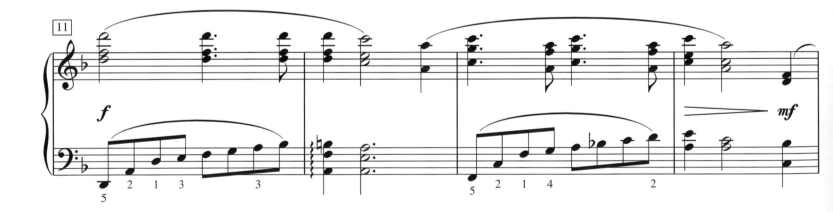

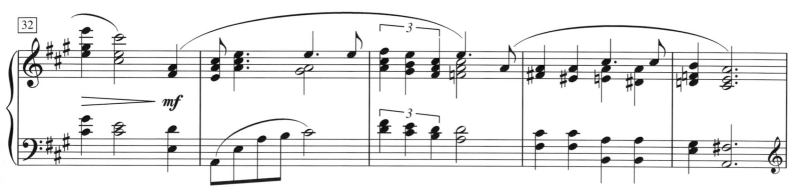

THERE IS A BALM IN GILEAD

African-American Spiritual
Arranged by Phillip Keveren

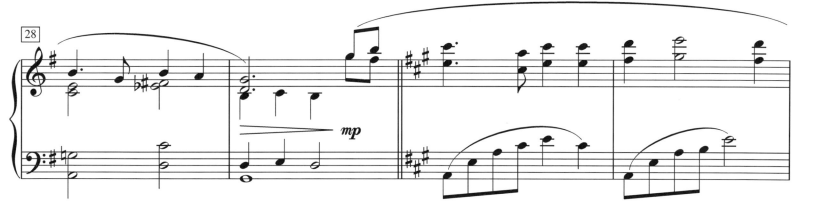

WAYFARING STRANGER

Southern American Folk Hymn
Arranged by Phillip Keveren

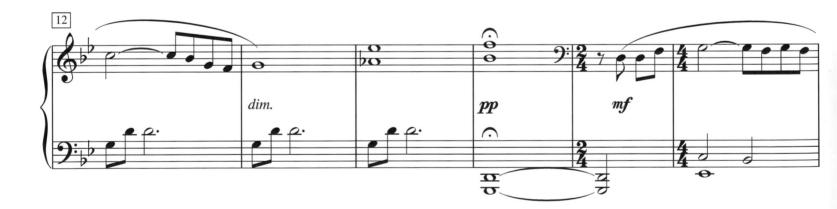

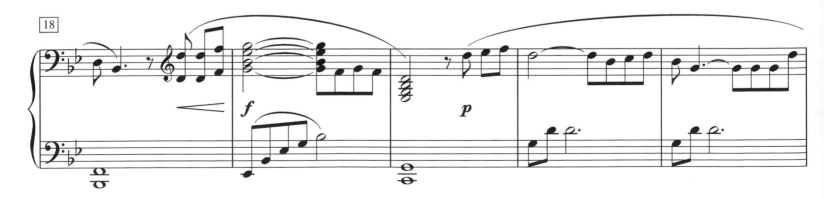

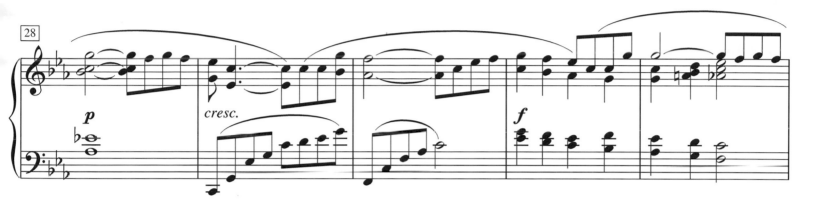

WERE YOU THERE?

Traditional Spiritual
Arranged by Phillip Keveren

Solemnly (♩ = 84)

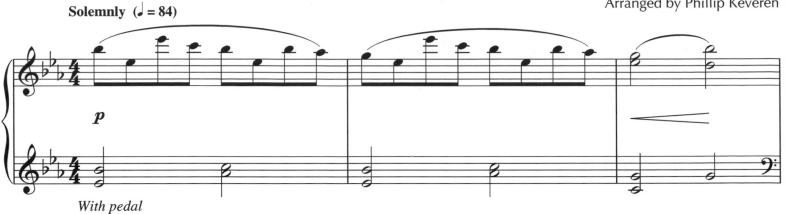

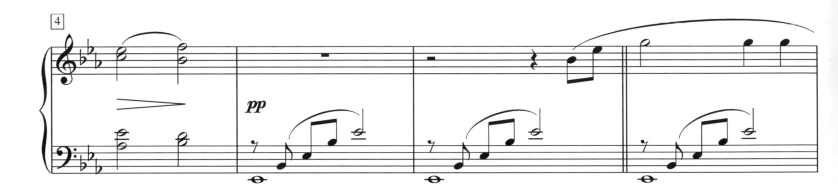

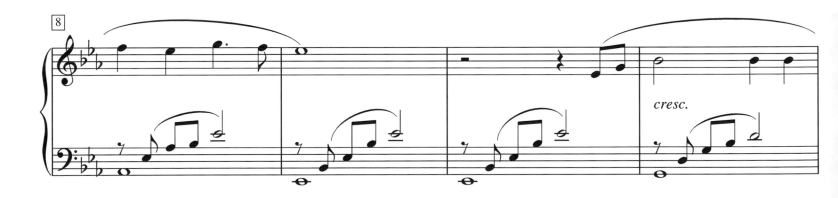

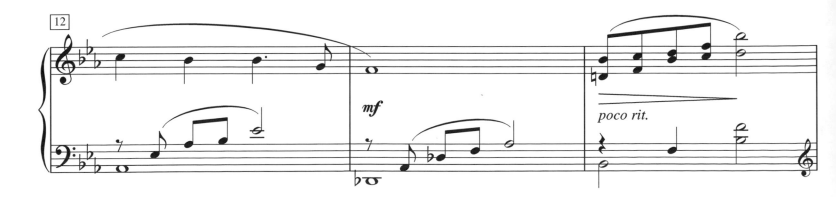

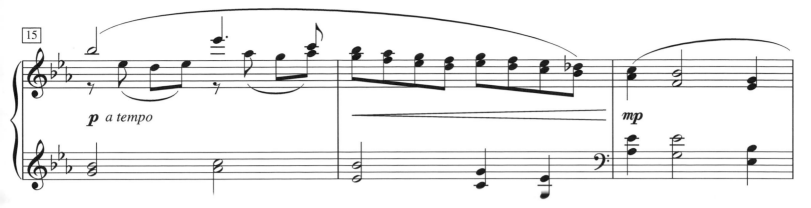

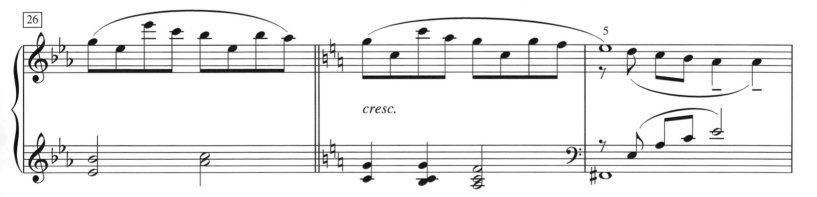

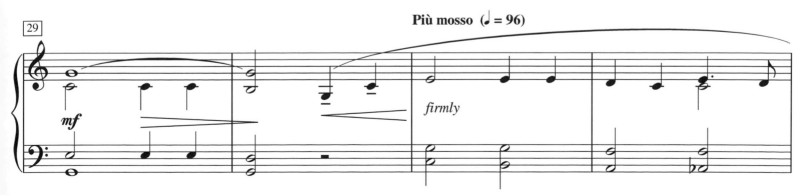

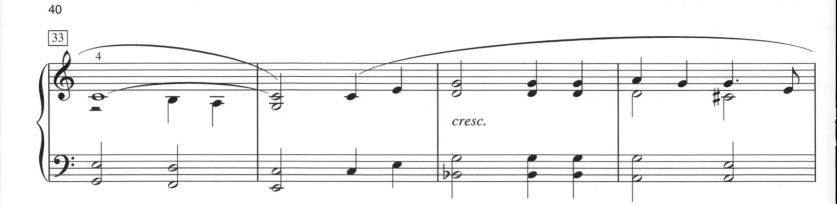

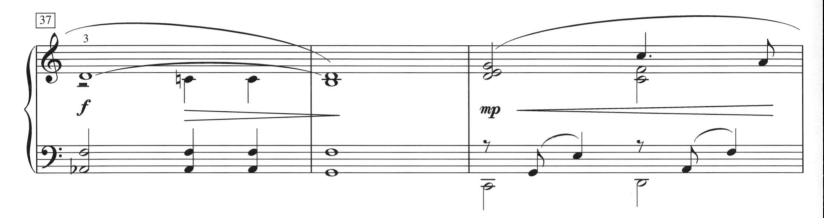

Tempo I (♩ = 84)

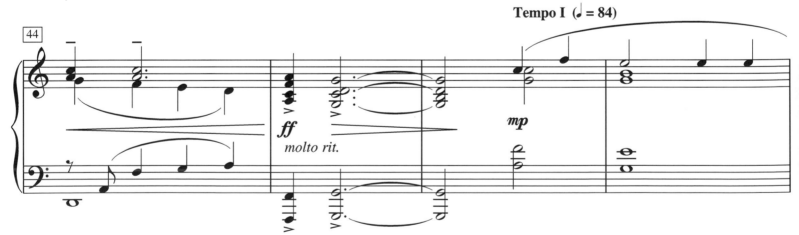

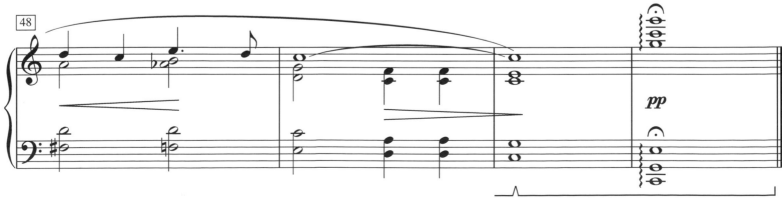